You're a survivor...
You're going to find strength
you didn't know you had
and grace to deal with
whatever comes along.

— Donna Fargo

The Strength of
Women

Words of Understanding
and Encouragement
for Survivors

Edited by Angela Joshi

Blue Mountain Press™
Boulder, Colorado

We gratefully acknowledge the permission granted by the following authors, publishers, and authors' representatives to reprint poems or excerpts from their publications: Susan Polis Schutz for "A woman is strength..." and "We don't often take the time...." Copyright © 1980, 1990 by Stephen Schutz and Susan Polis Schutz. And for "Love is the only true freedom...." Copyright © 1976 by Continental Publications. Renewed © 2004 by Stephen Schutz and Susan Polis Schutz. All rights reserved. Dutton, a division of Penguin Group (USA), Inc., for "Each precious moment of your life...," "Forgiveness is not about...," and "Asking for support..." from *Fearless Living* by Rhonda Britten. Copyright © 2001 by Rhonda Britten. All rights reserved. And for "I believe that suppressed emotion..." from "Opening the Can of Worms" from *Mother Warriors* by Jenny McCarthy. Copyright © 2008 by Jenny McCarthy. All rights reserved. Conari Press, an imprint of Red Wheel/Weiser, Newburyport, MA and San Francisco, CA, for "I think of cancer as a teacher..." and "I will not die an unlived life..." from *I Will Not Die an Unlived Life* by Dawna Markova. Copyright © 2000 by Dawna Markova. All rights reserved. And for "Love is one of...," "Forgiveness is a powerful act," and "Our power is greatly expanded..." from *Our Power as Women* by Helene Lerner-Robbins. Copyright © 1996 by Helene Lerner-Robbins. All rights reserved. And for "Imagine a Woman" from *Imagine a Woman in Love with Herself* by Patricia Lynn Reilly. Copyright © 1999 by Patricia Lynn Reilly. All rights reserved. And for "We need to know..." from *Women's Work Is Never Done* by BJ Gallagher. Copyright © 2006 by BJ Gallagher. All rights reserved. HarperCollins Publishers for "Take time for healing..." from *Journey to the Heart* by Melody Beattie. Copyright © 1996 by Melody Beattie. All rights reserved. And for "Having a good cry..." and "In the sunlight..." from *Choosing Happiness* by Alexandra Stoddard. Copyright © 2002 by Alexandra Stoddard. All rights reserved. And for "Refuse to fall down" from *The Faithful Gardener* by Clarissa Pinkola Estés. Copyright © 1995 by Clarissa Pinkola Estés. All rights reserved. Beyond Words Publishing, Inc., for "If you can't remember..." and "How can we recognize happiness..." from *Live in the Moment* by Julie Clark Robinson. Copyright © 2004 by Julie Clark Robinson. All rights reserved. Jonathan Van Meter for "If you haven't sat..." by Jennifer Aniston from "A Profile in Courage" (*Vogue*: April 2006). Copyright © 2006 by Jonathan Van Meter and Conde Nast Publications, Inc. All rights reserved.

Acknowledgments continued on page 92.

Library of Congress Control Number: 2009903442
ISBN: 978-1-59842-422-5

Blue Mountain Arts, Inc.
P.O. Box 4549, Boulder, Colorado 80306

Contents

A Strong Woman
Looks Inside to Find
the Strength She Needs

You are struggling right now.
Each day is a new challenge
with its own set of obstacles,
fears, and difficulties.
But you have taken the first step
toward starting fresh,
and you will overcome each obstacle,
conquer each fear,
and work through every difficulty.

You are strong of heart
and clear of mind.
Each day it is within you
to draw upon your strength
and rise above adversity.
Do not be afraid of what lies ahead
because you are not alone.

You will find your way...
little by little and day by day.

— T. L. DiMonte

There Is Strength in Knowing the Many Faces of Courage

Sometimes you will fight your way
through battle after battle
and show your strength and courage
by being a *warrior*.
Sometimes you will wait, listen to your heart,
find wisdom to take the right path,
and show your strength and courage
by being *patient*.
Sometimes you will stand up
for what you believe in,
say "no" to that which is not
compatible with your values,
and show your strength and courage
by being *true to yourself*.

Sometimes you will open new doors for yourself
even when you seem too tired to go on.
You will find the energy to see a new dawn—
a new point of view—and create a new
direction where none seems possible.
You will show your strength and courage
by being *optimistic*...
But no matter how many times
you are knocked down,
with strength and courage
you will always rise again.

— Bonnie St. John

A Survivor Lets Go of Fear and Lives Life to the Fullest

Each precious moment of your life in which you are frozen with fear is a moment when you are not being all you can be.

— Rhonda Britten

I will not die an unlived life.
I will not live in fear
of falling or catching fire.
I choose to inhabit my days,
to allow my living to open me,
to make me less afraid,
more accessible;
to loosen my heart
until it becomes a wing,
a torch, a promise.
I choose to risk my significance,
to live so that which came to me as seed
goes to the next as blossom,
and that which came to me as blossom,
goes on as fruit.

— Dawna Markova

Take Good Care
of Yourself

Take time for healing. Take time for what soothes your body, your mind, your soul.

Take a bath. Light a candle. Read a book. Take a walk. Get a massage. See your favorite healer if you desire. See a movie. Buy some flowers. Drink a cup of tea.

Sometimes we talk ourselves out of doing something healing for ourselves. We're too busy, too tired. But that is when we most need to take care of ourselves. Listen to your heart. What does it want? Listen to your body. What does it need? Trust what you hear.

— Melody Beattie

If you can't remember the last time you took a long nurturing bath, it's been too long. Let the world hold still for a little while. Maybe it's surrounding yourself in a warm and somewhat closed-in space—like the womb?—or maybe it's simply the task of taking care of yourself that results in a renewed feeling of "I'm OK." You step out, dry yourself off, and get back to whatever life is throwing at you.

— Julie Clark Robinson

Women are so good at taking care of others, but it's essential that we remember to take care of ourselves, too. Put yourself first when you need to... pamper yourself often. Nurse your wounds... nurture your dreams.

— Sara Emerson

A Survivor Recognizes True Strength

The woman who survives intact and happy must be at once tender and tough.

— Maya Angelou

You don't need to be the biggest,
loudest, or most forceful
to express true strength.
Instead, you must possess
a powerful spirit
that drives you forward
when there is no easy path.

Believe that you have
this strength in you—
even if you don't always
see it.

Adversity will not diminish it.
Turmoil will not hinder it,
and it will not fail you
when you need it most.

Believe that you
have the true strength
to face whatever lies ahead.

— Elizabeth Garlough

There Is a Lesson
to Be Learned
in Every Situation

When we learn from our pain, we transform from victims to victors, giving meaning to our suffering and breaking open to life's joyfulness as well as its sorrows.

— Mary Jane Ryan

Many times in life I have looked up at the sky and said aloud, "*Why* do I have to go through this?" It's clear to me now that everything has a reason and a purpose. Our job is to figure out what lesson we're supposed to learn from each experience and how to use it in our own lives or impart it to others.

— Sandra Lee

I think of cancer as a teacher that was not invited, but has come to my house to visit from time to time nonetheless. It sits on my left side whispering insistent questions that I cannot answer but still must explore.... What have I come here to give? What is unfinished for me to learn, to experience?

— Dawna Markova

Life is a series of levels,
cycles of ups and downs—
some easy, some challenging.
Through it all, we learn;
we grow strong;
we mature in understanding.
The difficult times are often
the best teachers, and there is
good to be found in all situations.
Reach for the good.

— Pamela Owens Renfro

Remember Your Power to Choose

When we realize that we always have choices—no matter how out of control things may seem—we suddenly find that we no longer feel helpless, but empowered.

— April Weston

Accept your power to make choices. Life is fluid with possibilities. Each of us has incredible power to shape our life and reshape our world. You can choose to have as magnificent a life as you want. Or you can choose to suffer magnificently. You alone choose how you react to what happens in life. And a lot happens, doesn't it? Just when life seems on track, we get slipped a pink slip. We answer the phone and get a medical diagnosis that fills us with terror. We see a loved one walk out the door, looking for love in all the wrong places. But remember your power. Honor your great ability to turn despair into hope. We can choose to transform the darkest of circumstances into the brightest of opportunities. We can choose to ask for help. We alone are responsible for the abundance of our day, for the depth of our suffering. Easier said than done? Absolutely. It requires gut-wrenching courage to accept responsibility for our own life, emotions, self-image, and well-being. But we never do it alone. We are always fortified with more support, light, and love than we could ever imagine.

— Susan Skog

Always remember, no matter what is going on in your life, it is your responsibility to choose how you respond. This does not mean you will not hurt. This does not translate to you should ignore what you feel. Not being a victim and taking responsibility means: feel the pain, honor the shock, look for the lesson, and keep on moving in a way that honors who you really are. You are Spirit in a body having a temporary human experience. Your experiences may knock you down, but it is your responsibility not to let them keep you down.

— Iyanla Vanzant

Each day I will remember...

I have choices
that I can take care of myself
and that it can be my first choice.

That it is okay to say no
whenever necessary
to stand up for myself,
then let it go!

That I do not have to please others
or be everything to everyone.
I do not have to be it all...
who I am now
is enough.

I can be honest and still be kind,
set boundaries and stick to them.
I can consider my own needs.

I will remember to honor myself,
that it is my responsibility
and divine right to do so...
each day.

— Pam Reinke

A Strong Woman Understands What It Means to Survive

Get through it. Cry if you must, bleed if you must, eat potatoes day after day if you must, but survive. Survive the disappointments that come at you like machine-gun fire. Survive on a diet of faith, hope, grit, and prayer. Get through it. Somehow, some way. Ask for help so you can survive. Ask for money, ask for food. Beg and plead if you must. Survive whatever they throw your way. Steel yourself, or collapse. Whatever you must do to survive, do it. Survive another hour, another day, another lifetime. Through the threats, survive. Through the pain, survive. For every woman who ever did and every woman who never could, you must, you will, survive.

— Rachel Snyder

The ones who survive in life do it by hammering at it one day at a time. You do what you have to do to get through today, and that puts you in the best place tomorrow.

— Oprah Winfrey

A Survivor Knows Who She Is

The closer you can connect to the heart of *who you are*—the fundamentals of your essence as a human being—the less likely you are to be thrown from your foundation when crisis hits. And after a crisis, the more rapidly you can reconnect with your own center, the more quickly you will get back on track....

The key to handling life's transitions—whether they be life-altering crises that change the course of our lives forever or the passages we all make from one phase of life to another—depends upon how well grounded we are in our own innate, natural abilities. Stop lamenting what you are not and celebrate *who you are!*

— Deborah Norville

Women are always being tested... but ultimately, each of us has to define who we are individually and then do the very best job we can to grow into it.

— Hillary Rodham Clinton

You are one of a kind—uniquely yourself—unlike anyone else. There are no two things in this universe exactly alike. No two trees, no two clouds, no two snowflakes, no two blades of grass, no two grains of sand are exactly alike, and there's no two of you even if you're an identical twin. You are the only "you" there is. Realize who you are, because you are more than enough.

— Judi Moreo

A Strong Woman Loves Herself

You can't control everything that happens in your life, but you can absolutely control how much love you give yourself. And when you are able to completely love the beautiful, unique woman that you are, you will have the strength to face any hardship.

— Alyssa Rienne

Love and accept yourself, no matter what it takes to come to that love. Love your body, mind, emotions, and spirit, whether they fit an ideal or not. Love your unique self. Love where you are now in your life and where you have been and where you are going.

— BettyClare Moffatt

You are lovable. You are deserving. You are enough. Trust your inner wisdom and trust that at your core there is goodness. Go beyond your self-imposed limits and make a commitment to living a life you love. Ask the universe for love and support. Ask God to fill you with compassion and strength. Face where you are at this moment and then move to higher ground. Grant yourself permission to have it all, you deserve it!

— Debbie Ford

Love is one of the greatest power expanders there is, for it brings us together on behalf of each other, makes us see unity in conflict, and forges bridges where there were none. Under the stress of everyday life, particularly in our quest to expand our power, we sometimes forget our natural impulse to love, which is always there. It needs only to be rediscovered.

— Helene Lerner-Robbins

Love is the power behind our resilience and optimism, the fuel for our wonder and curiosity, the essence of our joy, the core of our humor, the energy behind our music, the motivation for our work and play, and the penultimate lesson in our learning.

— Ronda Beaman, EdD

We are here only to love, and love casts out fear. When we understand that love is the reason for our power—that it *is* our power—we lose our fear of owning its strength. We become willing to experience the power within us, that it might be used as a channel through which love is expressed to all humankind.

— Marianne Williamson

Love is
the only true
freedom.
It lets us
cast off our
false exteriors
and be our
real
selves.

— Susan Polis Schutz

A Survivor Believes in Her Own Beauty

There is beauty
in so many unrecognized places.
It's a different beauty than
what you find in magazines,
where the faces all become the same
page after page.
Neither is it about shapes or fabrics
or cut and color.
Beauty is how you invite people
into your life and your heart no matter what;
it's when you laugh or cry with your whole self
just because that's how you feel.
Beauty is the way you move
when you think no one is watching
and you forget the shadows
of "should" and "supposed to."
Beauty is courage, energy, hope, and grace.
Beauty is you—
just the way you are.

— Sue Gillies-Bradley

Believe
you are beautiful;
cherish your
uniqueness
and be who you are;
through every hardship,
trust yourself
to overcome.
Be strong
when you can,
cry when you can't;
be wise of the past
and embrace now!
Reach out
when you are safe,
hide when you are not,
laugh often...
and listen carefully.
And never be afraid
to love yourself,
for that is where
all peace... is born.

— Pam Reinke

There Is Strength in Change

Change...
With a smile or a tear,
it touches our lives day in and day out,
the relentless, inevitable warrior of fate.
It can arrive at any moment in life,
but we must not feel threatened by it
or fearful.
Instead, when change is upon us,
we should open our eyes wider
with amazement and enthusiasm;
we should extend our arms further
and embrace the world around us.

Change...
Let it jolt you, push and pull you.
Let it challenge you.
Know in your heart that change
is what gives you the chance
to be yourself
and the opportunity to make your life
everything you want it to be.

— Deanna Beisser

Expect changes to occur, and realize that the power to make those changes comes from within you. Your thoughts and actions, the way you spend your time, your choices and decisions determine who you are and who you will become.

Life is an ever-changing process, and nothing is final. Therefore, each moment and every new day is a chance to begin anew.

— Barbara Cage

Life can change in an instant.
The struggles you face today
can become the victories
you celebrate tomorrow.

— Julia Mann

A Survivor
Practices Acceptance

Acceptance means that you
   can find the serenity within
to let go of the past
   with its mistakes and regrets,
move into the future
   with a new perspective,
and appreciate the opportunity
   to take a second chance.

Acceptance means that when
   difficult times come into your life,
you'll find security again and comfort
   to relieve any pain.
You'll find new dreams, fresh hopes,
   and forgiveness of the heart.

Acceptance does not mean
   that you will always be perfect.
It simply means that
   you'll always overcome imperfection.

Acceptance is the road to peace—
letting go of the worst,
holding on to the best,
and finding the hope inside
that continues throughout life.

Acceptance is the heart's best defense,
love's greatest asset,
and the easiest way to keep believing
in yourself and others.

— Regina Hill

Allow Yourself to Feel Your Feelings

We don't have to deny our emotions or bury our sadness when life takes a turn we hadn't wanted or expected. Sometimes events happen that bring us to our knees. Accept that this situation is making you feel emotions you have never felt before. Be loving with yourself. Feel your raw emotions, release them as you can, and move through the experience.

— Susan Skog

I believe that suppressed emotion causes disease, so the faster you start to FEEL, the faster you can HEAL.

— Jenny McCarthy

Remember that the first step in any healing process is always acknowledgment and acceptance of what is true right now. We don't heal anything by trying to block it out, get rid of it, or pretend it doesn't exist. We heal it by accepting that it's there, then becoming aware that there are other possible choices.

— Shakti Gawain

Good or bad, feelings need expression; they must be recognized and given freedom to reveal themselves. Put away the myth that says you must be strong enough to face the whole world with a smile and a brave attitude all of the time. You have your feelings that say otherwise, so admit that they are there. Use their healing power to put the past behind you, and realize those expressive stirrings in your heart are very much a part of you. Use them to get better, to find peace within, to be true to yourself.

— Barbara J. Hall

A Strong Woman
Cries Sometimes

Crying is the body's expression of release. Crying releases feelings of sadness, anger, pain. Crying is your body's acknowledgment of what you are feeling and thinking and enables you to begin to allow the grief to pass.

Give yourself permission to mourn.

— Elizabeth Johnson

Having a good cry can help us to heal.
We can feel sad about what is happening
or has happened and then move back into
the present moment. Breaking down in tears
over a seriously painful event is perfectly
natural and healthy. Think of your tears as
a sign of your compassion and love. Allow
yourself to be fully present to the pain. Feel
your emotions. Observe your thoughts. Your
tears will help to heal your broken heart. Let
your vulnerability be your strength. Tears of
sorrow cleanse your soul. Crying is a sign of
acceptance. You face the pain, you feel it in
your body, you observe it in your mind and
emotions. Crying doesn't last long. You catch
yourself, realizing it is now time to let go and
move on.

— Alexandra Stoddard

There Is Strength in Forgiveness

True forgiveness is good for the soul; it brings comfort to the heart, gives life new meaning, and offers hope. When we forgive ourselves and others, it opens up the pathway to such great peace... we wonder why we didn't walk this way before.

— Barbara J. Hall

Forgiveness is a powerful act. The process of forgiveness releases our power. As we forgive others, we become freer and more effective because we are not living our lives as a result of past injuries or injustices but choosing who we want to be in the present.

— Helene Lerner-Robbins

Learning to forgive ourselves and others is a breakthrough because it allows us to open up and become more compassionate. The state of our health and happiness depends on the healing power of compassion.

— Naomi Judd

Forgiveness is not about condoning the behavior or situation. Forgiveness overcomes the past, allowing you to move on, break free, and live in the present. Forgiveness takes our regrets and excuses and transforms them into lessons learned and skills acquired to help us achieve self-mastery.

— Rhonda Britten

A Survivor Takes Time to Relax and Heal

Relax... and let everything else
    fall into place.
Take one moment for you alone.
Let the day's trials roll off
    your shoulders.
Fill your head with thoughts
    of nothing at all.
And in that moment—
those brief few seconds where
    nothing matters—
breathe deeply and embrace the silence.
Truly relax, and when you wake
    to tackle life again,
remember this moment
and let it fill you with courage
    and serenity.

            — Deana Marino

Take time to let your thoughts drift, your muscles relax, and your dreams unfurl... Give yourself moments of absolute stillness to hear your wise inner voice and to heal.

— Susan Skog

Spend Some Time Alone

Use your alone time to...
enjoy quietness,
trust stillness,
feel the warmth of the sun,
and wrap yourself in love.
These are times of incubation—
trust them.
And when something moves in you,
nurture it gently
until you emerge
with your energy transformed
and a clear path ahead.

— Joanne Murphy

You know what happens if you're completely still? Your mind... that little tape that's running bup, bup, bup, all the noise... it eventually runs off the reel. And you have nothing left to think. And all of a sudden, the answers are just there.

— Melissa Etheridge

It is a difficult lesson today—to leave one's friends and family and deliberately practice the art of solitude for an hour or a day or a week.... And yet, once it is done, I find there is a quality to being alone that is incredibly precious. Life rushes back into the void, richer, more vivid, fuller than before.

— Anne Morrow Lindbergh

Surround Yourself with People Who Support You

According to Aristotle, we humans are biologically social animals and our "first nature" is to be around people. However, I personally discovered that after my trauma, being around people felt much more like my 2,841st nature. It's common to want to hide away. But studies show it's far more healthful to seek support.

— Karen Salmansohn

There comes a time in everyone's life where we can't move forward unless we rely on others. The people who know and love us *want us to ask*. Yet we ignore our need. We pretend that we'll get through on our own, and in the process, deny the frail reality of our humanity.

Too many of us would rather go it alone when help is available... just for the asking.

— M. Nora Klaver

Asking for support from the right people at the right time helps you summon the courage to show more of who you are to the world.

— Rhonda Britten

We don't make it alone in this world. We're lucky that there are people placed in our path to guide us, protect us, and touch our lives so that we can get through it all... one day at a time.

— Julia Escobar

A Survivor Finds Strength in Nature

Those who contemplate the beauty of the earth find reserves of strength that will endure as long as life lasts. There is a symbolic as well as actual beauty in the migration of the birds, the ebb and flow of the tides, the folded bud ready for the spring. There is something infinitely healing in the repeated refrains of nature—the assurance that dawn comes after night, and spring after the winter.

— Rachel Carson

If you're not able to get out and enjoy nature as much as you'd like, bring nature indoors. Buy some fresh flowers or a few potted plants; hang up a photograph of a beautiful nature scene where you'll see it often; open the windows and let in the fresh air and the sounds of the birds singing. Doing little things to bring nature to you can go a long way in lifting your spirits and soothing your soul.

— April Weston

Being outside in the natural world reminds us that we're but a speck of sand, which helps put our problems in perspective. G.O.D.—great outdoors—feels like nature's cathedral. The sights, sounds, smells, and textures also engage the senses and help to draw you out of self-absorption. When I feel like I'm in decline, it's rejuvenating to be surrounded by growth.

— Naomi Judd

My help is in the mountain
where I take myself to heal
the earthly wounds
that people give to me.
I find a rock with sun on it
and a stream where the water runs gentle
and the trees which one by one give me company.
So must I stay for a long time
until I have grown from the rock
and the stream is running through me
and I cannot tell myself from one tall tree.
Then I know that nothing touches me
nor makes me run away.
My help is in the mountain
that I take away with me.

— Nancy Wood

The Healing Power of the Sun

Remember to use all the available natural means of therapy and health maintenance. Sunlight is certainly one. Sunlight is the force that nourishes and energizes our bodies.

— Janet Luhrs

Enjoy the healing power of sunlight. Let it warm you outside and in; let it lighten your mood and make you smile.

— Kris McKenna

In the sunlight I open up like a flower, smiling. When I'm out in the bright sunshine I feel an inner calm, a contentment, a sense of the earth being kissed with grace. I thrive in the light, as we all do. Light to me is happy, and I make every effort to experience as much natural light as I can. After a rain, when the sun breaks through the clouds and I see those rays of divine light, my heart expands. I worship the sun, because it is our life force. We need it to live, and I need it to feel playful, young, and carefree.

— Alexandra Stoddard

A Strong Woman Has Faith

Faith isn't anything you can see;
it isn't anything you can touch.
But you can feel it in your heart.
Faith is what keeps you trying
when others would have given up.

Faith is trusting in a power
greater than yourself
and knowing that whatever happens,
this power will carry you through anything.
It is believing in yourself
and having the courage
to stand up for what you believe in.

Faith is peace in the midst of a storm,
determination in the midst of adversity,
and safety in the midst of trouble.
For nothing can touch a soul
that is protected by faith.

— Barbara Cage

If we can just let go and trust that things will work out the way they're supposed to, without trying to control the outcome, then we can begin to enjoy the moment more fully. The joy of the freedom it brings becomes more pleasurable than the experience itself.

— Goldie Hawn

Faith makes us certain of realities that we cannot see. I can't see the sun right now, but I can see the light. I can't see the wind, but I can feel it's there. I take one look up at the sail and there is no doubt. The storms will still come, the fear will still try to overtake me, but faith will sustain me. Faith—at first a gracious gift from God, it then becomes the muscle by which we can keep on trusting. No matter what happens, it is going to be okay.

— Nicole Johnson

Trust That You Will Get Through This

A new day is coming.
Celebrate your strengths—
you will be amazed
at how many you have.
Never let yesterday
stop you from living today.
No matter how long
the journey may be,
trust in your potential.
Things change; setbacks happen.
But in every hardship,
a new star shines.
Sometimes life can feel
like an uphill battle...
but you will reach the top.
And when you get there and look back,
the most amazing miracle of all
will be realizing
how many people
were standing there behind you.

There's no mountain
you can't climb;
no storm you can't weather.
You have the power of
the universe on your side.
You were made to soar—
and you are stronger
than you know.

— Linda E. Knight

A Survivor Knows
She Is Glorious and Strong

We don't have to do anything to be glorious; to be so is our nature. If we have read, studied, and loved; if we have thought as deeply as we could and felt as deeply as we could; if our bodies are instruments of love given and received—then we are the greatest blessing in the world. Nothing needs to be added to that to establish our worth.

— Marianne Williamson

I am a woman.
I hold up half of the sky.
I am a woman.
I nourish half of the earth.
I am a woman.
The rainbow touches my shoulders.
The universe encircles my eyes.

— Nancy Wood

A woman is
strength
tenderness
self-knowledge
self-confidence
mental alertness
sensitivity
body awareness
physical boldness
softness
not afraid
to be
today's woman—
a person
in full control
of herself

— Susan Polis Schutz

Imagine a Woman

Imagine a woman who believes it is right and good she is a woman. A woman who honors her experience and tells her stories. Who refuses to carry the sins of others within her body and life.

Imagine a woman who trusts and respects herself. A woman who listens to her needs and desires. Who meets them with tenderness and grace.

Imagine a woman who acknowledges the past's influence on the present. A woman who has walked through her past. Who has healed into the present.

Imagine a woman who authors her own life. A woman who exerts, initiates, and moves on her own behalf. Who refuses to surrender except to her truest self and wisest voice.

Imagine a woman who names her own gods. A woman who imagines the divine in her image and likeness. Who designs a personal spirituality to inform her daily life.

Imagine a woman in love with her own body.
A woman who believes her body is enough,
just as it is. Who celebrates its rhythms and
cycles as an exquisite resource.

Imagine a woman who honors the body of the
Goddess in her changing body. A woman who
celebrates the accumulation of her years and
her wisdom. Who refuses to use her life-energy
disguising the changes in her body and life.

Imagine a woman who values the women in
her life. A woman who sits in circles of women.
Who is reminded of the truth about herself
when she forgets.

Imagine yourself as this woman.

— Patricia Lynn Reilly

A Survivor Keeps Laughter in Her Life

Gotta have laughter.... Life isn't smooth, but you can survive the kinks and curves by laughing at them—and yourself.

— Maria Shriver

A good laugh provides a cathartic release, a cleansing of emotions, and a release of emotional tension. Even after the laughter has ended, body tensions continue to decrease. So the next time you're feeling sad or stressed, flash a big smile or give a hearty laugh. There's a lot of truth in the old adage, "Those who laugh... last."

— Joan Lunden

It is imperative that a woman keep her sense of humor intact and at the ready. She must see, even if only in secret, that she is the funniest, looniest woman in her world, which she should also see as being the most absurd world of all times.

It has been said that laughter is therapeutic and amiability lengthens the life span.

— Maya Angelou

Sometime when you have a free moment, write down what has given you joy in your life. What have you been happiest doing? What's been fun? What has made you laugh till you cried?... When you feel a lack of laughs in your life, look at your list and do one of the things on it. Put some of the joy back in.

— Maria Shriver

A Strong Woman
Never Gives Up

When you get into a tight place, and everything goes against you, till it seems as though you could not hold on a moment longer, never give up then— for that is just the place and time that the tide will turn.

— Harriet Beecher Stowe

Endure... Go through the darkness and come out the other side. When you think you can't stand another minute of this, know that you can. When you think you won't make it through another day, know that you will. When you can't take another moment of the pain and the fear and the feelings of hopelessness, take another moment anyway. Endure the heartache and come out heartstrong. Endure the tremors and the grief and the isolation and come out sturdy and robust and ready for another round. Like a diamond in the making, endure the heat and the pressure for what seems like eternity, and emerge with a new brilliance and clarity. When you think you've come to your end, dig deep and endure.

— Rachel Snyder

You gain strength, courage, and confidence by every experience in which you really stop to look fear in the face. You are able to say to yourself, "I lived through this... I can take the next thing that comes along."

You must do the thing you think you cannot do.
— Eleanor Roosevelt

You're a survivor. You're going to handle this. You're going to find strength you didn't know you had and grace to deal with whatever comes along. Pretty soon, you'll be on the other side, and it's just a matter of time until you will look back on this time in your life and draw strength from the knowledge that even though the road was rocky, you persevered and carried on.
— Donna Fargo

Refuse to fall down.
If you cannot refuse to fall down,
refuse to stay down.
If you cannot refuse to stay down,
lift your heart toward heaven,
and like a hungry beggar,
ask that it be filled,
and it will be filled.
You may be pushed down.
You may be kept from rising.
But no one can keep you
from lifting your heart
toward heaven—
only you.
It is in the midst of misery
that so much becomes clear.
The one who says nothing good
came of this,
is not yet listening.

— Clarissa Pinkola Estés

There Is Strength in Positive Thinking

I believe a positive outlook affects you physically and research has shown that patients with a positive outlook do better.... Your thoughts are like tire tracks in the dirt. You make the tracks deeper each time you drive over them, so it's best not to have the same negative thoughts every time. Start afresh and go down a clear road.

— Olivia Newton-John

Optimism is a happiness magnet. If you stay positive, good things and good people will be drawn to you.

— Mary Lou Retton

When we use positive perception to interpret what we see, we avoid falling prey to doom and gloom. If we can look beyond today, its challenges and obstacles, we can create a better tomorrow. If we can see, it must come to be.

— Iyanla Vanzant

Never Let Go of Hope

Hope is the sun rising; it's rain after a drought; it's finding a cure when you thought there was none; it's an answered prayer. Hope is seeking out solutions and second chances, and always believing with all your heart that things will get better...

Hope is the most important promise you can ever make to yourself. Keep it and you will always have peace.

— Juliet Pivens

The human spirit is amazing. Somehow hope springs eternal even under the bleakest of conditions.

— Fran Drescher

Hope is such a marvelous thing.
It bends, it twists, it sometimes hides,
but rarely does it break.

Hope sustains us when nothing else can.
It gives us reason to continue
and the courage to move ahead
when we tell ourselves
we'd rather give in.

Hope puts smiles on our faces
when our hearts cannot manage.
Hope puts our feet on the path
when our eyes cannot see it.
Hope moves us to act when our souls
are confused by the direction.

Hope is a wonderful thing—
something to be cherished and nurtured
and that will refresh us in return.
It can be found in each of us,
and it can bring light into
the darkest of places.

— Brenda Hager

Heal Through Creativity

Brushing paint in back-and-forth strokes, dipping a calligraphic pen in an inkwell, punching out shapes, and peeling off stickers all supply a tactile distraction in which the hands are busy and the mind is free. In this precise place of mental liberation, and out of this realm of inaudible expression, a healing balm is concocted from your own artistic well and applied, not just to paper, but to your soul.

— Sharon Soneff

Get out your paper, your paint, your clay and begin to explore your self, your memories, the paths of your heart. Don't worry about the end result. Through the process of expressing your creativity, you may find yourself, perhaps without even trying, more resolved in your heart and in your life. Lighter. Freer. Soaring on the wings of self-expression.

— Kelly Rae Roberts

Doing creative activities doesn't simply distract us from our struggles; it can actually help us overcome them. In a creative space, we can work through feelings, discover solutions to problems, spark new passions, and begin to heal our wounds.

— Alyssa Rienne

Let the Hard Times Help You Appreciate the Good Times

Every crisis offers a treasure trove of information about ourselves. (That's why they call it an *emergency*—you *emerge* and *see*.) A crisis prompts us to raise our consciousness and choose to open up to more of who we're meant to be. It also shows us just how many more dimensions there are to living. In the Chinese language, the word "crisis" is made up of two characters, depicting "danger" and "opportunity." It's always up to you and me to choose, at every crossroads, which path we take.

— Naomi Judd

How can we recognize happiness if we have nothing to compare it to? In a way, I almost enjoy the down times because life has taught me that later everything will work out and I'll soar again. In other words, don't be too hard on the bad times. They serve you well—later.

— Julie Clark Robinson

If you haven't sat in the dark depths of sadness and pain—you can't appreciate feeling good.... I really believe that everything is meant to be.

— Jennifer Aniston

Often, the truly great and valuable lessons we learn in life are learned through pain. That's why they call it "growing pains." It's all about yin and yang.... They're the positives and negatives of life. One doesn't exist without the other. How you experience your pain, what you learn from it, and how you live through it— that's what makes all the difference.

— Fran Drescher

A Survivor Is Connected to Other Women

Our power is greatly expanded when we support one another, both at work and in our personal lives. As one of us faces a seemingly impossible challenge or achieves some new goal or struggles with the process of discovery, we all benefit. By sharing our experiences with each other, we get stronger both individually and as a group, and we pave the way for those who will come after us.

— Helene Lerner-Robbins

If we stick together there's so much
we can accomplish, because no matter
what the struggle, as long as you've got
somebody, you can make it.

— Jennifer Hudson

I want to remind you of the importance
of your spirit and how indelibly connected
we all are. Our spirits crave union and we
have much to share with each other. Write
down this sentence somewhere where you
can see it often: I am indelibly connected
to everyone.

— SARK

A Strong Woman
Values Friendship

We owe it to ourselves as women to cultivate
our friendships, encourage each other's dreams,
and understand our commonality. It is through
these bonds that we find our true selves.

— Lisa Crofton

Friends are the multicolored cloaks we wear, the
circles we draw around us, the chores we share,
the letters we wait for, the gifts we want to buy,
the heartaches we take on as our own, the place
we turn with our fears, our wants, our sadness....
Who knows what needle takes what thread and
seams two people together. There is nothing less
tangible than friendship and very little so potent.

— Beth Kephart

We need to know
    we're not alone.
We need to hear
    that other women
    share our experiences.
We need reassurance
    that there's someone who understands—
someone who's been there, done that.

As women, we take turns
    encouraging, supporting,
        and cheering one another on.

— BJ Gallagher

Know That You'll Make It Through

How do you make it through? You take it one day at a time. You face your fears. You keep your promises. You deal directly with your challenges. You get the best possible help and care. You turn to caring, positive people you know will be there for you.

You believe. You take steps to change what needs changing. You talk it over. You laugh. You go ahead and cry. You pray. You stay involved. You live the best life you can today. And when tomorrow comes, you do it all over again.

You hang in there. You hold on tight to your hope. You never let go. You know, deep down inside, what a special person you are. And no matter what comes along, you never forget it. You stay strong. You keep the faith. And you make room for the brighter day that, someday soon, is going to shine so much serenity back into your life.

— Anna Tafoya

There Is Strength in Gratitude

It seems to me, of all the bright sides to life's disasters, gratitude is the brightest, the one that emits the purest pleasure. To feel grateful if you're religious is to feel blessed. To feel grateful if you're not religious is to feel lucky. Either way, it's the sort of feeling that, at its height, makes you practically hurt with joy. Gratitude is life's best present, no doubt about it.

— Betty Rollin

Gratitude unlocks the fullness of life. Gratitude makes things right. It turns what we have into enough, and more. It turns denial into acceptance, chaos to order, confusion to clarity. It can turn a meal into a feast, a house into a home, a stranger into a friend. It turns problems into gifts, failures into successes, the unexpected into perfect timing, and mistakes into important events. It can turn an existence into a real life, and disconnected situations into important and beneficial lessons. Gratitude makes sense of our past, brings peace for today, and creates a vision for tomorrow.

— Melody Beattie

When things go wrong, you've got to believe you will get through them and focus on the positive things in your life.

I've had bad moments of depression, but I've always reminded myself I have a lot to be grateful for.

— Olivia Newton-John

We don't often
take the time out of
our busy life
to think about all
the beautiful things
and to be thankful for them
If we did
reflect on these things
we would realize how very
lucky and fortunate we really are

— Susan Polis Schutz

A Survivor
Has Patience

The Dalai Lama said, "If you want others to be happy, practice compassion. If you want to be happy, practice compassion."

In other words, don't pressure yourself to recover too fast.

After a traumatic event, time seems to move in slow motion. Each week will feel like seven. You feel trapped in limbo, where everything is out of your control.

Do not be impatient about your progress or impractical either.

Months after the event, you might think you should be feeling much better. But realize the healing process has no timetable.

— Karen Salmansohn

As any gardener will tell you, the cycles of nature require patience. You can't just plant a seed and expect it to flower the next day. You can't tug on the leaves or unfurl the bud to hurry the process. Even a fast-growing vegetable like a radish requires time.

So do we. When we practice patience, we come more into alignment with the natural rhythms of life. We remember that "to everything there is a season," and we stop pushing for life to be different than it is. Winter takes as long as it takes, but it always ends—and so does summer. That's the law of nature.

— Mary Jane Ryan

Waiting patiently asks us to allow life to move through and transform us as we bend like cattails in the wind, twisting and turning but somehow surviving.

— Mary Jane Ryan

Know That You Deserve
All the Happiness in the World

I believe that we are so unaccustomed to living in joy that we actually create suffering and wrap it like a familiar cloak around ourselves. We forget that it is our right and privilege to live in a state of joy. Be willing to notice just how much joy you're creating and living with.

— SARK

I kept looking for happiness, and then I realized: This is it. It's a moment, and it comes, and it goes, and it'll come back again.

— Nicole Kidman

When you sense a faint potentiality for happiness after such dark times you must grab onto the ankles of that happiness and not let go until it drags you face-first out of the dirt—this is not selfishness, but obligation. You were given life; it is your duty (and also your entitlement as a human being) to find something beautiful within life, no matter how slight.

— Elizabeth Gilbert

Joy is our goal, our destiny. We cannot know who we are except in joy. Not knowing joy, we do not know ourselves. When we are without joy, we grope in the dark. When we are centered in joy, we attain our wisdom. A joyful woman, by merely being, says it all. The world is terrified of joyful women. Make a stand. Be one anyway.

— Marianne Williamson

Emerge

And the day came when
the risk to remain tight in a bud
was more painful
than the risk it took
to blossom.

— Anaïs Nin

Come out of the shadows and come into your own. Leave behind your armor and your shells and your veils and your protection, and emerge fresh and newly born. Today, step from behind your screens and masks. Peel away the layers upon layers of fear and emerge into a world of love and trust. Emerge in your own time, in your own way, with your chosen guides at your side. See the world through the eyes of the woman you were always destined to be. Like a tiny chick cracking her way out of a darkened egg, emerge. Like a radiant butterfly, like a glorious rose opening from a tightly closed bud, emerge. Out of your past and into the gift that is your present, emerge. When it's time, when you're ready, emerge.

— Rachel Snyder

There Is Strength in
a New Beginning

It isn't always easy to make changes, but
there's no better advice than this: just do
your best. Make sure you stay strong enough
to move ahead, because there are some
wonderful rewards waiting for you.

It won't all make sense right away, but over
the course of time, answers will come,
decisions will prove to be the right ones,
and the path will be easier to see. Here are
some things you can do that will help to see
you through...

You can have hope. Because it works wonders
for those who have it. You can be optimistic.
Because people who expect things to turn out
for the best often set the stage to receive a
beautiful result.

You can put things in perspective. Because some things are important, and others are definitely not.

You can remember that beyond the clouds, the sun is still shining. You can meet each challenge and give it all you've got.

You can count your blessings. You can be inspired to climb your ladders and wish on stars. You can be strong and patient. You can be gentle and wise.

And you can believe in happy endings. Because you are the author of the story of your life.

— Kelly Lise

Choose to Be...
a Woman of Strength

Choose to be well in every way. Choose to be happy no matter what. Decide that each day will be good just because you're alive.

You have power over your thoughts and feelings. Don't let your circumstances dictate how you feel.

Even if you don't have everything you want, even if you're in pain or in need, you can choose to be joyful no matter what you're experiencing. You are more than your body, your physical presence, and your material possessions. You are spirit. You have your mind, heart, and soul, and there is always something to be thankful for.

Decide that life is good. Decide to enjoy today. Decide that you will live life to the fullest now, no matter what.

Trust that you will change what needs changing, but also decide that you're not going to put off enjoying life just because you don't have everything you want now. Steadfastly refuse to let anything steal your joy. Choose to be happy, choose to be a woman of strength... and you will be!

— Donna Fargo

ACKNOWLEDGMENTS (continued)